AN OCEAN
FOOD CHAIN

AN OCEAN FOOD CHAIN

ODYSSEYS

A. D. TARBOX

CREATIVE EDUCATION·CREATIVE PAPERBACKS

Published by Creative Education and Creative Paperbacks
P.O. Box 227, Mankato, Minnesota 56002
Creative Education and Creative Paperbacks
are imprints of The Creative Company
www.thecreativecompany.us

Design and production by Blue Design
Art direction by Rita Marshall
Printed in the United States of America

Photographs by Alamy (Brian Atkinson, Alissa Everett, Leslie
Garland Picture Library, Stephen Frink Collection), Getty
Images (Altrendo Nature, Robert Arnold, Pete Atkinson, Fred
Bavendam, Aldo Brando, Nick Caloyianis, DEA/A. CURZI,
David Doubilet, Jeff Foott, Johner, Alex Misiewiez, Chris
Newbert, Flip Nicklin, Paul Nicklen/National Geographic,
Silvia Otte, Kevin Schafer, DR & TL Schrichte, Gail Shumway,
Stephen St. John, Thayer Syme, Patrick Trefz, D. P. Wilson/
FLPA, Art Wolfe, Norbert Wu)

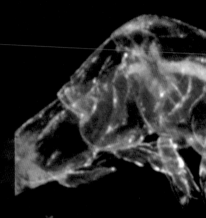

Library of Congress Cataloging-in-Publication Data
Tarbox, A. D. (Angelique D.)
An ocean food chain / A. D. Tarbox.
p. cm. — (Odysseys in nature)
Summary: A look at a common food chain in the Pacific
Ocean, introducing the plankton that starts the chain, the killer
whale that sits atop the chain, and various animals in between.
Includes bibliographical references and index.
ISBN 978-1-60818-541-2 (hardcover)
ISBN 978-1-62832-142-5 (pbk)
1. Marine ecology—Pacific Ocean—Juvenile literature. 2. Food
chains (Ecology)—Juvenile literature. I. Title.

QH541.14.T37 2015
577.7'4—dc23   2014038229

CCSS: RI.8.1, 2, 3, 4; RI.9-10.1, 2, 3, 4; RI.11-12.1, 2, 3, 4

First Edition HC 9 8 7 6 5 4 3 2 1
First Edition PBK 9 8 7 6 5 4 3 2 1

Cover: California sea lions
Page 2: Steller sea lions
Pages 4–5: Krill
Page 6: A tropical ocean coast

CONTENTS

Introduction

A bird swoops through the sky. In the depths of the sea, a whale dives. A wolf runs for miles across a snow-covered plain. They fly, swim, and travel in search of food. Animals spend most of their time looking for a plant or animal to eat, which will nourish them, provide energy, or help their offspring survive. A food chain shows what living things in an area eat. Plants, called producers, are the first link

OPPOSITE: Gulls are large seabirds found along ocean coasts. They squawk noisily as they search for such food as fish, crustaceans, and even garbage.

on a food chain. Consumers, or animals that eat plants or other animals, make up the other links. The higher an animal is on the food chain, the less energy it receives from eating the animal below it. This is why there are more plants than plant eaters, and even fewer top consumers. Most animals eat more than one kind of plant or animal. Food webs show all of the possible food chains within a wildlife community.

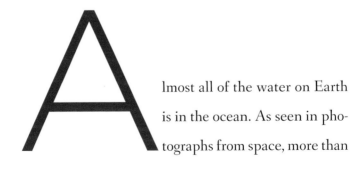

Almost all of the water on Earth is in the ocean. As seen in photographs from space, more than

70 percent of the planet is covered in water. The ocean is such a vast place that it qualifies as four different zones: the intertidal zone near the shore; the pelagic zone in the open water; the benthic zone deep in the ocean; and the abyssal zone at the bottom. Of the 20 million different creatures on the planet, only 250,000 of them live in the ocean. However, the ocean remains the world's least-explored environment, and scientists are discovering new ocean plants and animals all the time. There are five oceans: the Atlantic, Pacific, Indian, Arctic, and Antarctic. They are all connected, but each ocean has its own unique collection of plants and animals. The plants and animals that live off the shores of the Pacific Ocean make up numerous food chains, including one that begins with microscopic plankton and ends with a black-and-white "whale."

Plankton: Puny Plants and Bitsy Beasts

The ocean is mostly a cold place, with an average temperature of 36 °F (2.2 °C). Near Antarctica, the ocean temperatures are below freezing. The only reason the ocean does not turn to solid ice is because of all the salt in the water. Yet the ocean is not cold everywhere. Near underwater volcanoes in the Pacific, the ocean can be more than 500 °F (260 °C)—hot enough to burn flesh. And on the ocean surface near warmer climates such as the tropics, the temperature may feel as comfortable and warm as bath water.

Most of the salt found in the ocean is the same salt that people add to their food at the dinner table. As much as a third of the salt used for human consumption is taken from the ocean. There are 80 other substances in ocean water, including dissolved quantities of silver and gold. The salt in the ocean comes from dissolved salts in rocks and soil, which is carried by rivers to the sea.

The ocean is in constant motion because of **tides**, waves, and **currents**. The moon's **gravity** causes high and low tides about every 12 hours. Wind produces most ocean waves, although underwater earthquakes and volcanoes can also create waves. Sometimes the energy released from an earthquake causes a tsunami, a giant wave that travels across the ocean and can strike land thousands of miles away. In 1958, a tsunami hit Alaska. The wave was the tallest ever recorded, reaching more than 1,700 feet (518 m) into the sky, higher than the tallest building then in existence.

Currents can influence the climate near coasts and help animals, such as eels, move to other parts of the ocean. They act similar to a flowing river by moving water at the ocean surface or in the ocean depths. Strong winds, proximity to land, and Earth's rotation help determine the direction in which currents flow. Some currents are caused by the amount of salt in the water. Cold, salty water is denser than warm water and sinks, causing deep ocean currents. These deep ocean currents can be found where there are a lot of icebergs freezing and thawing, such as near Antarctica.

Brains and Brawn

Dolphins are famously smart mammals, but they also have amazing physical capabilities, using their strong tail fins, called flukes, to leap, twist, and flip out of the water, as well as to swim at speeds of up to 25 miles (40.2 km) per hour. Their rubbery skin covers about an inch (2.5 cm) of blubber and helps them keep warm. It also gives them a little protection from large sharks that try to prey on them. To defend themselves, dolphins may use their strong nose like a torpedo, ramming the shark in an attempt to chase it away or kill it. Dolphins occasionally eat small sharks, but they mostly prey on small fish and squid. Squid are cephalopods that can grow longer than 32 feet (9.8 m). Some sperm whales bear scars that tell of attacks by giant squid. Dolphins do not feed on the giant squid, but they locate small squid species using echolocation. When a squid spots a dolphin, it squirts black ink and tries to propel itself away.

The Pacific Ocean is the largest of the 5 oceans and covers 64 million square miles (166 million sq km), from the western side of North America to Asia. It is also the deepest ocean, reaching down almost seven miles (11.3 km) at its lowest point, the Mariana Trench. The Pacific holds about twice as much water as the second-largest ocean, the Atlantic. Much of the Indian Ocean is in the tropics and contains coral reefs. The Arctic and Antarctic (sometimes known as "Southern") oceans are small and cold.

Perhaps the most important life forms found in all oceans are plankton. Plankton are made up of phytoplankton, microscopic plants so tiny that more than a million of them can fit in a cup of water, and zooplankton, a number of very small marine animals. The tiny plants and animals drift with currents and waves and go in and out with the tides.

Phytoplankton are similar to plants on land in that they make their own food by **photosynthesis**. The tiny plants can be found at the water's surface and at depths where there is light (the sun's light usually disappears in the ocean after depths of 600 feet, or 183 m). When there is not enough sunlight, some phytoplankton capture and consume **bacteria**, zooplankton, or larger phytoplankton. Unlike land plants, phytoplankton do not have roots to anchor them to a spot, and many have small tails called flagella that help them move around on the surface or dive.

The ocean often looks blue because it reflects the color of the sky. However, where there are large congregations of phytoplankton, the ocean can look green. Some phytoplankton cause parts of the ocean to glow in the dark. A so-called red tide occurs when harmful bacteria in the phytoplankton bloom. This often causes illness or death to the fish, ocean mammals, and birds that feed on them.

Zooplankton survive by eating phytoplankton. Unlike phytoplankton, which stay close to the surface for light, zooplankton often dive to the depths of the ocean during the day and return to feed on phytoplankton at night. Zooplankton can dive to depths so far below the surface that the pressure would crush human lungs, yet the zooplankton are not affected. Scientists think that the tiny creatures make this daily, back-and-forth **migration** to escape from **predators** such as basking sharks, blue whales, or seahorses. The zooplankton are able to handle the water and temperature changes (the water gets colder at greater depths) because they are made mostly of water. Whether the plankton are floating at the ocean's surface or on their way down, though, many of them will not escape the jaws of a certain school-traveling fish.

Sardines: Plentiful School Fish

Most people are familiar with the sardine as the little fish packaged in tin cans at the grocery store. A sardine's body can be as small as four-fifths of an inch (2 cm) long, but most **species** are a few inches in length. Young herring, pilchard fish, and the true Pacific sardine living in the Pacific Ocean are all sold as sardines. Found swimming off of ocean coasts throughout the

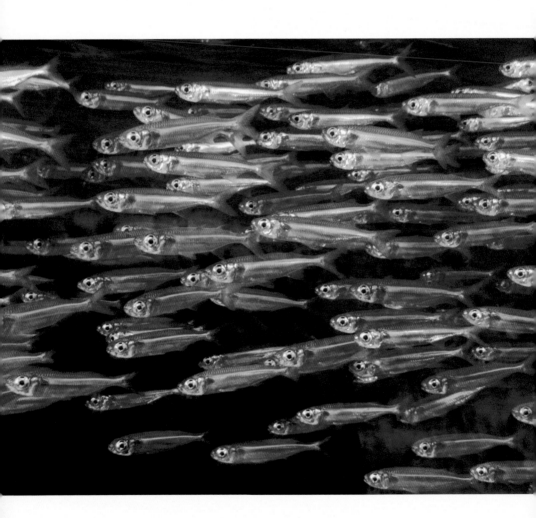

world (except in the cold polar seas) and covered in silvery scales, the sardine is wider at the center and tapered at the head and tail. Muscles make up most of the sardine's weight, and strong muscles in its tail fin propel it through the water. Ocean water is 500 times heavier and thicker than air, yet a sardine can swim through it with graceful ease. The ocean contains only three percent of the oxygen found in air. Sardines are able to get dissolved oxygen from the water by passing water through their **gills**, which collect the oxygen and add it to the fish's bloodstream.

Found along every **temperate** or **tropical** coast, sardines have many enemies, including albatrosses, bottlenose dolphins, and copper sharks. Sardine numbers are considered abundant in most parts of the ocean, but some species of sardines are endangered, or at risk of extinction, because of overfishing. Sardines are short-lived fish, rarely

Fragile Gardens

Coral reefs may look like colorful underwater gardens, but they are not plants. Reefs are composed of the skeletons of tiny animals called coral polyps. The polyps live inside the garden-like structures and make them from calcium carbonate, a mineral they draw into their bodies from the ocean. Reefs are usually found in warm, shallow waters and are easily killed if the water temperature becomes a few degrees colder or warmer. Every December, around the equator, a warm ocean current called El Niño replaces the cool ocean water for a few months. It becomes an El Niño year if the ocean temperature is raised more than 1 °F (0.6 °C) for six months. Some scientists think global warming has made El Niños stronger, more frequent, and able to stretch beyond the equator to the eastern Pacific Ocean. El Niño has been blamed for recent coral deaths. Warmer water has turned many colorful coral reef gardens into white graveyards. As corals die, they lose their beautiful colors. Some corals are now extinct, due largely to El Niño and pollution.

living past three years of age. Depending on the kind of sardine, spawning—the depositing of eggs—might take place seasonally or throughout the year.

A female sardine may release as many as 30,000 sardine eggs every 15 days. Most sardines, such as the Pacific sardine, release their eggs in the ocean, but some sardines migrate away from the ocean's salt water to a freshwater river to deposit their eggs near the water's surface, where males fertilize them. The Pacific sardine's tiny eggs are about 0.04 inch (1 mm) across and

Waves can be generated by different causes, including wind, earthquakes, and gravity. Even large waves have little effect on the sea creatures below them.

float at the ocean's surface with the plankton. When the eggs hatch, baby sardines called larvae drift and feed on the plankton for several months. When they reach about the size of a large paper clip, their internal organs and outer dorsal fin shift, and they soon are adult sardines.

Sardines travel together and feed on plankton in large schools that—in some places and at certain times of the year—can reach lengths of up to a mile (1.6 km)! Because so many sardines can be found together at the same time, it is easy for fishermen to capture them in nets. The Pacific sardine, which for hundreds of years was the most abundant fish off the coast of North America, became a victim of too much netting in the 1940s. Sardine numbers plummeted, and it took years after laws were passed to protect them for sardines to make a comeback. Their numbers are now high enough to once again be fished.

Almost every year, a fascinating sardine phenomenon known worldwide as "The Greatest Shoal on Earth" occurs off the eastern coast of South Africa. From May to July, scuba divers, researchers, and nature enthusiasts flock to South Africa to see what many call the most spectacular marine event on the planet: a sardine run. Not only do millions of sardines gather during this time, but thousands of ocean predators such as whales, dolphins, seabirds, and sharks also congregate to feed on the little fish. It is a rare chance to watch ocean food chains in action.

Gentle Giant

Fin whales are today endangered due to overhunting for their oil and meat. To better understand fin whales and make sure they continue to thrive, researchers take people out on whale watching trips off the coasts of North America and elsewhere to study and increase interest in whales. Fin whales are a lot like horses: they are intelligent, have eyes on the sides of their head, and graze most of the day. Even though fin whales are the world's second-largest animal, reaching lengths of 87 feet (26.5m), they feed on the smallest creatures in the ocean, such as plankton, shrimp, and small fish, using the **baleen** in their mouth to capture these tiny creatures. Fin whales have superb hearing and can hear other whales from hundreds of miles away. Human ears can't hear fin whale songs; scientists have to use special underwater microphones to listen to fin whale communication. Despite the endangered status of the fin whale, countries such as Iceland, Norway, and Japan continue hunting the whale.

Researchers are still trying to figure out why so many sardines annually gather in such enormous schools, but they have noticed that there is an upwelling of nutrient-rich, cool water near South Africa's eastern coast about this time of year. This upwelling provides ideal conditions for phytoplankton to bloom, and the phytoplankton are an important food source for sardines. The food and cooler water temperatures (57 to 68 °F, or 13.9 to 20 °C) attract the sardines. If the water temperature is more than 68 °F (20 °C), the sardines will not run up the South African coast, the predators will not congregate, and, for that year, the spectacular marine event is canceled.

Ichthyologists, or fish scientists, who study sardines have found that the small fish use their sense of smell to find their favorite foods. After locating plankton, sardines open their mouth and devour their tiny targets whole. Through all life stages, from larvae to adult, sardines feed on plankton. As they do so, though, they have to be careful, for the ocean is also home to a bigger fish with a taste for sardines.

Pacific Salmon: The Great Migrator

Fossil remains suggest that salmon have been swimming in the ocean for almost 100 million years. There are several species of salmon in the Pacific Ocean, and they are distinguished from other fish by the curved shape of their mouth, their sharp, angular teeth, and their adipose fin, a fatty fin located between their dorsal and tail fins. Their forked tail helps them swim close to shore or in the middle of the

OPPOSITE: The red salmon, also called the sockeye salmon, is one of the most common Pacific salmon species. It features the beak-like jaw characteristic of the fish.

ocean, glide through fast-flowing rivers, and make leaps from the water. Salmon can reach lengths of more than 5 feet (1.5 m) and weigh as much as 105 pounds (47.6 kg).

Salmon have a narrow tube called a **lateral line** that runs from their gills to their tail. It helps them to detect vibrations caused by approaching predators such as dolphins or to identify objects in dark ocean water. The salmon's silvery scales are coated by a slime layer that helps protect them from disease and allows the fish to slip through water as if greased in oil.

The salmon know which river or stream to go to by their memory of its smell.

In the winter, when salmon are usually ready to breed, they leave the ocean and head to freshwater rivers, sometimes migrating thousands of miles to get to the streams of their birth. The salmon know which river or stream to go to by their memory of its smell. During their migration, they undergo changes because they do not eat. Their mouth and teeth elongate, and their silvery scales disappear. Depending on the species of salmon, their skin becomes thicker and changes color, sometimes to a blood red. Once in the river, they travel up to 30 miles (48.3 km) a day and sometimes can be seen leaping out of the water, clearing obstacles such as logs or trying to escape the claws of grizzly bears that wade into the rivers to grab them.

Once the salmon arrive at their spawning grounds in the river or stream, the females use their strong tail to dig a place in the sand and deposit their eggs. The nest may be as deep as 18 inches (45.7 cm), and the eggs inside may number into the thousands. Male salmon spread milt, a white substance from their body, onto the eggs to fertilize them. The females immediately bury the nest with their tail and make another with the same

Misunderstood Killer

People have tried, but great white sharks have never survived longer than a couple of days in captivity. The huge sharks are also difficult to study in the ocean because observations have to be made from a shark cage for safety. Great whites can grow more than 23 feet (7 m) long and weigh more than 7,000 pounds (3,175 kg). Like all sharks, their skeleton is made of cartilage, a soft, flexible material like that found at the end of the human nose. Of the approximately 50 to 80 shark attacks that happen globally every year, up to half of them are blamed on great whites. Great whites do sometimes eat people, but they normally hunt seals, dolphins, squid, and fish, including other sharks. Many people misunderstand the important role great whites have in the ocean. The big sharks prey on the old and weak and help clean up the ocean by eating large dead animals such as whales. Because their jaws sometimes sell for thousands of dollars, great white sharks are endangered in many parts of the world.

number of eggs. Salmon will do this over many days, and then, within hours or a few days, they die because they have not eaten and have used up all their strength.

Weeks later, the buried salmon eggs hatch, and the young fish that emerge are called alevin. From their bellies hang yolk sacs, which will feed the newborns for the next few weeks. When the salmon are about an inch (2.5 cm) long, they grow scales and start drifting in the river's current toward the ocean. As they travel, they undergo more physical

When salmon decide to leave the ocean, they never turn back and will try to fight their way past any obstacle.

changes: their upper scales become a bluish color, and their inner organs start adjusting to the salt water. Few salmon make it to the ocean, most being eaten along the way by other fish. Those that do survive will stay in the ocean for up to five years, until a winter day when they feel the urge to return to the place where they were born and spawn, continuing the salmon cycle.

Salmon migration is an interesting **instinctual** behavior. When salmon decide to leave the ocean, they never turn back and will try to fight their way past any obstacle. Even when salmon reach a dam, their instinct is to do all they can to get over it. They leap and hurl themselves

Migrating Pacific salmon undergo a grueling voyage. They may swim thousands of miles and leap up strong rivers, only to die after they reach their nest and spawn.

at the dam but cannot pass it and soon die, battered and bloodied. Some slip into the dam's turbines and are chopped and shredded. **Salmon ladders** built near dams, such as those on the Columbia and St. Joseph rivers, are meant to help salmon get across and help their young return to the ocean, but they don't always work well.

O nce safely in the ocean, young salmon grow fast and become large because of all the food available, such as shrimp and sardines. Sardines swim in schools as a way to protect themselves and increase their chance of survival, but this also makes it easy for salmon to locate them. Plunging into the schools, salmon use their sharp teeth to pluck the sardines off like grapes and swallow the little fish whole. With each salmon attack, the school of sardines reacts by fleeing and then quickly huddling again like a giant flag rippling in the wind. Salmon can grow big by snatching lots of sardines, but there is a playful creature in the ocean that grows into a true heavyweight by catching salmon.

A sea lion's best chance when facing killer whales is to swim for the shore. If it cannot reach land, it likely will become one more link on the ocean food chain.

Sea Lion: Smart Surfer

Easily trained and gregarious, sea lions have delighted people for years as part of entertainment acts and as wild creatures commonly seen near piers. These marine mammals can be quite vocal with their doglike barks and are amusing to watch as they bob their heads and surf waves. Male sea lions, called bulls, are much larger than females. There are five

Especially large sea lions weigh as much as 2,400 pounds (1,089 kg) and can be as long as a small car.

species of sea lions, and all bulls have a blockish chest and a thick neck. Most have a mane of long hair that extends from the back of their head to their shoulders. Especially large sea lions weigh as much as 2,400 pounds (1,089 kg) and can be as long as a small car. Both bulls and females have wide flippers for swimming, tipped with claws. They have 34 sharp teeth perfect for tearing into fish and whiskers around their mouth that help them feel for food in dark water.

Sea lions can be found near the coasts of South America, southeastern Asia, and western North America. Wherever they live, sea lions spend a lot of time in the ocean, where they hunt for food, but they go ashore to breed, give birth, nurse their young, and rest. Most sea lions are polygamous, which means the bulls mate with several females. Bulls sometimes fight each other over breeding territories and may go up to three months without eating so as not to lose their females to other males.

Sea lions are rarely alone. When in the ocean, they swim in groups of a dozen or more, and when ashore, there may be thousands of them on a single beach. Sometimes they spend several days at sea diving for food and surface only for short breaks and air. They have been

known to dive as deep as 1,760 feet (536 m) and to stay underwater for as long as 40 minutes.

Because sea lions can be taught to perform certain tricks and behaviors, they are used not only in entertainment but in some cases have been trained by militaries to find and retrieve items such as missiles from the ocean floor by attaching a line to them. Sea lions can also be taught to communicate with humans by sign language, much like chimpanzees and dolphins are able to do. Human ears are not capable of hearing some of the sounds sea lions make underwater. The loud barks that humans can

TAKEAWAY

Sea lions can also be taught to communicate with humans by sign language ...

hear are usually meant to threaten or show dominance to other sea lions. A young sea lion can also recognize its mother's sounds. Vocal recognition is an **adaptation** to living in such large colonies.

Young sea lions play a lot on land and in the water. They wrestle underwater and chase each other on land, and the young males sometimes practice fighting by slamming their bodies into each other. Another favorite pastime of sea lions is surfing waves; like human surfers, the animals have been seen

Sea lions like to rest after a big meal and may flop down side by side on a beach and sleep for as long as 12 hours after feasting on salmon or other fish.

catching waves and riding them almost all the way to shore. Diving back into the water before reaching the beach, the sea lions sometimes repeat this bodysurfing trick over and over.

Sea lions also have a reputation as thieves and have been known to steal fish from fishermen's nets. In the ocean, they eat a variety of sea animals, including eels and squid, as well as fish such as salmon. Near the North American coasts, sea lions seem to know when salmon will make their annual migration back to rivers to spawn. They place themselves in the best positions to snatch the salmon before they leave the ocean or meet them farther upriver.

Once a salmon is caught in a sea lion's jaws, the sea lion may thrash the fish on a rock or other surface to kill it. Many a sea lion has been seen tossing its fish high in the air and then catching and eating it. It is not unusual for a sea lion to play with its food before it eats it or with pieces left over after it has eaten some of it. But when playing with a salmon dinner, a sea lion in ocean waters needs to remain watchful, because a very large and clever predator may be lurking nearby.

Killer Whale: Ocean Wolf

Killer whales, also known as orcas, are found in all oceans of the world. They live in groups called pods and are easy to identify by their head, which is shaped like the front of an airplane, their large size (30 feet, or 9.1 m, in length), and their distinct black-and-white coloring. They weigh more than large elephants and are long-lived; males can live up to 60 years and females up to 90.

OPPOSITE: Killer whales are capable of leaping completely clear of the water. They are also the fastest mammals in the sea, able to reach speeds of 35 miles (56.3 km) per hour.

Blowholes function much like a nose and allow the whale to take in air without lifting its head completely out of the water.

Killer whales have a distinct dorsal fin that is located approximately halfway down their body in the middle of their back. In males, the dorsal fin is tall and mountain-shaped, reaching heights of six feet (1.8 m). The dorsal fin on the female is smaller and shaped more like an ocean wave. Killer whales are mammals with large flippers, which they use to steer and maintain balance. Most mammals on land have lots of hair to keep them warm, but killer whales do not. Instead, their thick, rubbery skin is lined with four inches (10.2 cm) of fat to help retain body heat.

A killer whale breathes through a blowhole located at the top of its head. Blowholes function much like a nose and allow the whale to take in air without lifting its head completely out of the water. When it exhales, it sends a large mist of water called a blow into the air. The blowhole closes as the killer whale leaves the surface and goes to depths of around 200 feet (61 m), where it can stay submerged for up to 12 minutes at a time.

Female killer whales often start new pods and are sometimes the leaders. The other members of the pod are her offspring and their children. Males slip away from their pod for short periods to mate with a female from another pod. Mating usually takes place in the summer but can occur at any time of the year. After about an 18-month pregnancy, a newborn killer whale, called a calf, is born tail-first. The mother pushes the calf up to the surface for air, and then the calf drinks milk from slits in her belly. Young killer whales become adults at about 10 years old, the age at which they start to breed.

Killer whales often spyhop, or lift their bodies out of the water, take a look around, and then lower themselves. Scientists think that the whales spyhop to search for prey such as seals. Sometimes killer whales also lobtail, or lower their head in the water, raise and wave their tail several times, and then strike their tail against the ocean's surface, sending spray

A pod of killer whales is a fearsome hunting force. They have been known to kill and eat other whales, sea lions, penguins, and even moose swimming near ocean shores.

in every direction. This might be done to scare fish into clumping together so that it will be easier for the whales to feed on them.

Killer whale pods may include as few as 2 or as many as 30 members. Sometimes multiple pods will travel and hunt together for short periods of time and number up to 500. Usually, killer whales stay with their pod for life and are very sociable, constantly communicating with one another through body signals and sounds. Their sounds

TAKEAWAY Killer whales are often described as the wolves of the sea because of their intelligence, communication, family structure, and hunting tactics.

include whistles and squeaks, and a clicking noise is used to echolocate prey such as salmon.

Killer whales use teamwork when hunting. Depending on the prey, the hunt may end in seconds (as in the case of sea otter prey), or it may take hours (as in the case of an attack on a gray whale). Killer whales are often described as the wolves of the sea because of their intelligence, communication, family structure, and hunting tactics. They have been known to kill polar bears and even great white sharks. A 2,000-pound (907 kg) sea lion is a nice meal for killer whales and helps meet their 500-pound (227 kg) daily food requirement. But a sea lion won't go down without a fight and will use its sharp teeth and claws to defend itself if it cannot successfully flee to land.

When a sea lion is spotted, the pod of killer whales tries to block the animal's escape. The whales take turns striking the sea lion with their tail flukes or ramming it with their heads. Sometimes a sea lion is killed quickly because it is taken by surprise, but it can take up to two hours before a large sea lion weakens enough to be snatched by one of the killer whales, taken underwater, and drowned. The dead sea lion is then eaten, with every member of the pod getting a share.

The sea lion in the killer whale's belly is connected to the salmon, the sardine, and plankton in the ocean food chain. When the whale dies, perhaps from **polychlorinated biphenyl (PCB)** poisoning, its body will float to the bottom of the ocean, where **scavengers** and bacteria will break it down, providing nourishment for new plankton, and the ocean food chain will begin again.

Slow Walker, Fast Swimmer

Instead of teeth, sea turtles have sharp ridges that line their mouth. They use these ridges to slice through prey such as jellyfish. Their sense of smell is believed to be better than that of a dog, and although they move slowly on land, sea turtles can swim as fast as 20 miles (32.2 km) per hour in the ocean. Unlike land turtles, sea turtles cannot pull their head or legs into their shell. The largest sea turtle, the leatherback, does not even have a hard shell. Leatherbacks are sometimes up to 8 feet (2.4 m) long and can weigh as much as some whales—about 1,500 pounds (680 kg). Their favorite prey is the box jellyfish. Some kinds of box jellyfish, such as the ones found near Australia, contain enough venom to kill 15 people. The leatherback is immune to jellyfish venom, however, and it chomps the floating jellies like candy. Tiger sharks, which reach average lengths of 14 feet (4.3 m), eat leatherbacks. Because of past overfishing and the high mortality of their eggs,

Selected Bibliography

Arnold, Caroline. *El Niño: Stormy Weather for People and Wildlife*. New York: Clarion, 1998.

Brennan, Patricia. *Sea Turtles and Other Shelled Reptiles*. Chicago: World Book, 2002.

Cerullo, Mary M. *Sea Soup: Phytoplankton*. Gardiner, Maine: Tilbury House, 1999.

Ferrari, Andrea, and Antonella Ferrari. *Sharks*. Buffalo, N.Y.: Firefly Books, 2002.

Hirschi, Ron. *Salmon*. Minneapolis: Carolrhoda Books, 2001.

Sayre, April Pulley. *Ocean*. New York: Twenty-First Century Books, 1996.

Walker, Sally M. *Dolphins*. Minneapolis: Carolrhoda Books, 1999.

Glossary

adaptation
a change an animal species makes over time—such as growing thicker fur or eating other foods—to survive in its environment

bacteria
microscopic, single-celled organisms that can live in the soil or water or inside animals and plants; some bacteria are helpful to their host, but others are harmful

baleen
fringed, stretchy, hornlike material that hangs from the upper jaw of some whales and strains plankton from the water

cephalopods
marine animals such as octopuses and squid that have long tentacles, a large head and eyes, and a beak

currents
continuously fast-moving sections of ocean water that flow in one direction

echolocation
the process of locating prey by sound waves that are usually sent from an animal's head and echo back to tell it the location and identification of nearby animals or objects

gills
organs found in marine animals such as fish that allow them to take dissolved oxygen from the water

gravity
the invisible force between celestial masses (such as Earth and the moon) that pull on objects (such as the ocean) as they rotate

instinctual	describing a natural reaction to a situation without being told or taught what to do
lateral line	sense organs on the sides of animals such as fish that allow them to detect vibrations
mammals	backboned animals that have hair and nurse their young with milk
migration	the movement from one climate or location to another to find food or to breed
nutrient	minerals, vitamins, and other substances that provide an organism with what it needs to live, grow, and flourish
photosynthesis	a process by which plants exposed to sunlight are able to make their own food
polychlorinated biphenyl (PCB)	an industrial toxic chemical that builds over time in the tissues of animals, resulting in their illness or death
predators	animals that live by killing for their food
salmon ladders	man-made structures of concrete or wood placed near dams to help migrating fish pass through the dams so they can return to their spawning grounds in rivers and streams or back to the ocean
scavengers	live animals that feed on dead animals
species	animals that have similar characteristics and are able to mate with each other

temperate	characterized by a moderate temperature, without lengthy periods of hot or cold
tides	daily rises and recessions of the ocean due to the gravitational pull of the moon
tropical	characterized by year-round temperatures above 64 °F (17.8 °C) and frequent rainfall

Index